ARTS EDUCATION FOR A
MULTICULTURAL SOCIETY
An Evaluation of the AEMS Project

Edited by John Eggleston

$t\!b$

Trentham Books

First published in 1995 by Trentham Books Limited

Trentham Books Limited
Westview House
734 London Road
Oakhill
Stoke-on-Trent
Staffordshire
England ST4 5NP

British Cataloguing in Publication Data
A catalogue record for this book is available from the
British Library.

ISBN: 1 85856 050 0

Designed and typeset by Trentham Print Design Ltd., Chester
and printed in Great Britain by Bemrose Shafron (Printers) Ltd.,
Chester.

iv

Contents

Acknowledgements   ix

Introduction   xi

Chapter One   1
THE GENESIS OF AEMS

Chapter Two   7
AEMS REGIONAL DEVELOPMENT

Chapter Three   13
AEMS IN THE SCHOOLS
South Glamorgan, Walsall and Cheshire

Chapter Four   37
AEMS AND FURTHER EDUCATION
Dewsbury, Walsall and Huddersfield

Chapter Five   59
CONCLUSIONS

Chapter Six   65
OVERVIEW

AEMS will need to do what no predecessor has done. It will need to pay detailed attention to the history of multicultural and antiracist arts projects including its own. It will need to review the success and failures of philosophy in action and the value and limitations of artists' placements in schools.

Professor Nick Stanley, Birmingham Polytechnic speaking at the AEMS Exhibition, Duniya Ki Ankhe, 1990.

Acknowledgements

This report has been compiled from a range of sources. They include the work of AEMS co-ordinators and the Cheshire researchers and the voices of teachers, pupils and students. Helen Dennison was contracted to undertake much of the original evaluation and her work has been extensively used and is gratefully acknowledged. Extensive use has been made of material generated by Maggie Semple, Project Director. John Eggleston, who chaired the evaluation of the Project and who was also a member of the Project Steering Committee throughout its duration, has augmented and edited the report.

It has also been possible to draw on a number of documents produced by local authorities who hosted the project. Two of them are available in published form: *Arts Education for a Multicultural Society* by Alison Haynes, Walsall Metropolitan Borough Council, 1992) and *An Arts Policy for Kirklees Schools* (Kirklees Metropolitan Council, 1994). A detailed evaluation study of one of the areas involved; 'Midshire', is being produced independently — *Celebrating Naivety: The Role of Black Artists in Multicultural and Anti-Racist Education* (London: David Fulton, 1995).

The financial support of the Arts Council of England is gratefully acknowledged; this has made the publication of this document possible.

Acknowledgements

Introduction

Arts Education for a Multicultural Society (AEMS) was established in 1987 to:

Explore and develop ways of giving effect to existing multicultural/anti-racist education policies, and encourage multicultural awareness in the arts curriculum.

Initiated by the Arts Council of Great Britain, the Commission for Racial Equality and the Caloustie Gulbenkian Foundation, the project ran for three and a half years, establishing partnerships with local education authorities, schools, colleges and regional arts associations. At a later stage the Further Education Unit became a partner, and a separate chapter reports on what was achieved in the further education sector. AEMS produced and disseminated information and resources ranging from a Directory for Arts Education for a Multicultural Society, GCSE Literature packs and, through its regional groups, a variety of multicultural and anti-racist handbooks and video materials, to support and enhance the arts curriculum.

AEMS organised a national training programme for Black and cultural minority artists to prepare them for a proactive role in education. It worked with more than 80 schools and colleges, co-ordinated over 1000 visits by artists and attracted 'challenge' funds from Regional Arts Associations (now redesignated Regional Arts Boards) and LEAs totalling £331,460 by the final term of 1989-90.

Evaluation Aims

The aim of the evaluation report is to identify the achievements of AEMS and to answer questions in three areas. The first is multicultural curriculum practice. What knowledge, skills and experience are necessary to deliver a multicultural arts curriculum in schools and colleges?

How far was the development plan a useful strategy document for the co-ordinators working in widely different education authorities? How were the expected and unexpected demands on the co-ordinators met by in-service training, and the organisational support of AEMS itself? Since multicultural education incorporated anti-racism, what were the particular skills needed to challenge overt discrimination or racist responses?

The second area concerns policy and philosophy. The evaluation shows the impact of LEA policy after partnership with AEMS. The evaluation sought specific examples of initiatives in arts and education which would not have happened without AEMS. The policy enquiry also sought evidence on strategies to continue what AEMS had begun, either through provision of funds to pay co-ordinators and continue artists' residencies, or to find new contexts for AEMS work in the changing the educational climate.

The third level of achievement is artist development and training. AEMS played a key role for many crafts-people, sculptors, painters, musicians, artists, poets, writers, story-tellers and dancers, creating new networks and helping artists develop their potential as teachers and animators in a formal education situation. The evaluation assesses the extensive training programmes for educators used to introduce them to political concepts of anti-racism and cultural diversity, and the programmes for Black and ethnic minority artists who were to become catalysts of change for teachers and students.

The evaluation casts a critical eye on the theoretical framework for AEMS ideas and attempts to assess how far this framework has informed the practice of addressing racist and Eurocentric attitudes within school institutions. As a summative evaluation, focus has been given also to the organisational structure and AEMS strategies of training, monitoring, evaluation and dissemination. As a major focus, the evaluation puts in context its achievement for the education and arts professions; it also considers how models of best practice may be replicated and developed.

Chapter One

THE GENESIS OF AEMS

In 1980, the Arts Council, the Caloustie Gulbenkian Foundation and the Commission for Racial Equality held conferences in five cities on 'Arts Education for a Multicultural Society', attracting artists, educators, local authority and arts association officers, academics and community arts organisations.

Iaon Reid, then Assistant Director of the Caloustie Gulbenkian Foundation recalls:

> On the one hand, great enthusiasm was expressed for the creation of multiculturalism and the unique role that the arts could play in its development within the education system. On the other hand teachers and educationalists openly admitted they lacked skills in this area, and the knowledge to find out where to discover appropriate artists and resource materials. Artists expressed frustrations at the level of finance and at the lack of understanding of their art form. (*AEMS Magazine*, 1989)

Five years later, the three funding agencies commissioned research to identify developments and problems in multicultural arts education in Birmingham, Cardiff, Glasgow, Manchester and London. In February 1986, Helga Loeb and Maurice Plaskow reported that the arts of ethnic minorities did not form part of a planned curriculum in secondary schools; while within primary schools, the main reference to multicultural arts was usually only through festivals and celebrations.

The Loeb and Plaskow report was not published. Described by one senior officer as 'lacking an ideological framework', it reflected the confusions, hopes and fears of many educators searching for answers on multiculturalism, racism, art and the goals of education itself.

Education Authorities and 'Education for All'

As the vision for AEMS drew nearer to reality in the minds of the funding agencies, many education authorities had attempted to integrate approaches of equal opportunities and multicultural education, albeit with varying degrees of commitment and understanding.

These actions were prompted by an influential report by a government committee, chaired first by Anthony Rampton (1981) and later by Lord Swann (1985). The Committee of Inquiry had been established in 1979 to investigate causes of the under-achievement of children of West Indian origin and to propose remedial action. The Interim Report (of Rampton) made an unprecedented claim that:

> ..racism, both intentional and unintentional, has a direct and important bearing on the performance of West Indian children in our schools. *Interim Report,* Rampton Committee, (1981) Chapter 2, para 4, p 12)

Multicultural education was proposed in the final Swann Report as the means through which children could understand their own society and the cultures and ethnic identities of others. The report presented a range of curriculum examples of multicultural education, notable for their exclusion of the arts and inclusion of humanities and religious studies. The multicultural education policy of Berkshire was seen as a model and provided substantial examples of curriculum approaches and resources. Critics of the Swann Report felt that too great an emphasis was laid on tackling racism through 'tolerance and understanding' of minorities, rather than attending to inherent racism and inequalities of power within education institutions themselves.

Black and Ethnic Minority Artists

In order to realise the 'broad heterogeneous curriculum which draws positive advantage from different cultural traditions' AEMS was to play a unique role in preparing Black and ethnic minority artists as catalysts and positive role models in education. As educationalists were responding to the educational failure of many children and the political pressure for education to answer for the series of inner city disorders of the 1980s, the creative expressions of Black and cultural minority artists were slowly achieving recognition across the country.

A burgeoning infrastructure of theatre and dance companies, musicians and poets working with new or traditional forms was first brought to public attention by Naseem Khan in her report, *The Arts Britain Ignores* (1976). Khan concluded that these arts were underfunded and marginalised. Six years later, helped by the political commitment shown by the Inner London Education Authority between 1982 and 1986, the development of a Black visual arts movement, led by Eddie Chambers and Keith Piper, was raising awareness of exciting and challenging work. In 1985 the Arts Council was funding just three Black clients. By 1987-88 this had increased to 32 clients.

The Arts in Schools — A Model for AEMS

The model of a national curriculum development project was derived, to a great extent, from the *Arts in Schools* project. Drawing on the rationale for arts education in the Caloustie Gulbenkian Report, *Arts in Schools* (1982), it established partnerships with 18 education authorities to support drama, dance, visual and verbal arts across primary and secondary education.

The central team comprised a director, two project officers, an administrator and information officer. Their roles combined support of regional groups and analysis, publication and dissemination of the project's materials.

The Formation of AEMS

By July 1986, the informal steering committee, comprising Godfrey Brandt, then Education Officer at the Arts Council, Robbie Robinson of the Commission for Racial Equality and Iain Reid of the Caloustie Gulbenkian Foundation, had created a new curriculum development body, AEMS.

3

The chief objectives were to:

- [ ] provide information, resources for teachers, LEAs and artists;
- [ ] establish training initiatives;
- [ ] establish models of good practice to be monitored and evaluated.

By April 1987, the first co-directors of the project were appointed to work for three days each on the project. Housed at the Arts Council's offices in London, the team faced two urgent tasks: first to establish a National Committee and, second, to construct a Development Plan to represent the objectives and describe the envisaged basis of LEA partnerships.

The National Committee

The first national steering committee meeting was held on 21 October 1987. The funding body representatives were joined by a distinguished panel of academics, artists and senior advisers.

The committee was to meet monthly to manage the project, process partnership applications, raise funds and oversee the development of in-service teacher training and the production of resources. The seniority of some members within education structures helped to ensure an effective voice on emerging areas of concern, such as the terms of reference and membership of the new National Curriculum groups.

Several members had overseen the Arts in Schools project; others came with considerable experience of anti-racist work in politics and education.

The AEMS Development Plan

The Development Plan of April 1988 was intended to maintain the debate on anti-racist and multicultural education through an arts-derived agenda.

Drawing on the work of the Swann Committee (1985) the plan took as its starting point the current emphasis on multiculturalism as the co-existence and mutual respect for, and understanding of, different cultures. This was important because it marked a positive recognition of the contribution made by minority groups over the centuries. It regarded the question of racism and the role of schools and colleges in relation to it as a central issue. It believed that the most significant long term approach towards tackling the problem lay in the development of a multicultural curriculum especially in the arts which involved life-styles and attitudes and epitomised the essence of different cultures.

Racism would be tackled by arts education in three ways,

- ☐ the promotion of wider knowledge and understanding of different cultures;

- ☐ the location of pupils' immediate environment within a national and international context;

- ☐ in-service training to promote awareness, the dissemination of knowledge and the clarification of policy.

The creative opportunities offered by AEMS to partners were intended to realise multicultural policies and to encourage multicultural awareness in the arts curriculum.

Strategy

AEMS intended to respond to areas of need through research and dissemination by:

- ☐ setting up research curriculum development projects;

- ☐ establishing training programmes for teachers and artists;

- ☐ providing access to resources, information, materials and skilled people.

Both regional and national advisory groups would be involved in monitoring and evaluation, documentation and dissemination. AEMS also intended to create a national forum to debate and share experiences and information about good practice.

Partnerships

The Development Plan prescribed partnerships between Arts Associations, LEAs, artists and community representatives. The institutional partners were expected both to support regional programmes financially, and to manage the affairs of the local groups. The Plan recommended that up to four schools and one teacher education college in each region should be identified. Two staff should also be designated from each AEMS school. Having outlined the minimum in-service training requirements to qualify regions for AEMS participation,

LEAs were expected to fund 24 one-day workshops, two weekend workshops for staff, and the artists involved in the project. AEMS also recommended that an advisory teacher be seconded to act as regional co-ordinator and evaluator of the project.

Dissemination

A team approach to 'strategic multicultural arts development' throughout each authority was proposed by AEMS. The Plan emphasised the importance of giving information to parents, governors and Parent Teacher Associations.

Support for regional conferences, exhibitions of work during and at the end of the project, was also to be funded by the authorities.

The Role of Regional Arts Associations

AEMS suggested that support of ethnic minority artists should lead to their involvement in other programmes of work of the Regional Arts Associations (subsequently RABs) who were expected to collaborate in artists' training programmes.

The Timetable

A timetable was outlined in detail for training, negotiations, commissioning of research, and the organisation of projects. The pilot AEMS programme was expected to run over four school terms.

The first development plan was circulated to authorities in April 1988; a revised version was prepared for the Steering Committee and became the strategy document of AEMS from mid-1988.

References

AEMS Magazine, Summer 1989

'Rampton Report', (1981) *The Interim Report of the Committee of Inquiry into the Education of Children from Ethnic Minority Groups*, London: HMSO

'Swann Report' (1985) *Education for All, The Final Report of the Committee of Inquiry into the Education of Children from Ethnic Minority Groups*, London: HMSO

Naseem Khan (1976) *The Arts Britain Ignores*, London: Community Relations Commission, 1976. The report led to establishment of MAAS (Minority Arts Advisory Service), a number of regional arts service agencies, and a monthly bulletin *Echo*

Calouste Gulbenkian Foundation (1982) *Arts in Schools. Principles, Practice and Provision*, London: Calouste Gulbenkian Foundation

Chapter Two

AEMS REGIONAL DEVELOPMENT

The lesson was led by a Chinese dancer from the AEMS project. It combined dance, music and mime and led to pupils observing and then participating in a range of dance activities exploiting the capacity of their bodies for expressive and disciplined communication. Pace, delivery and context were excellent in this session.

Provision is both rich and challenging and generates an active creative response of high quality, through the presence of professional artists in the classroom.

HM Inspectorate Report, *A Survey of Arts Provision in the Royal Borough of Kingston upon Thames*, March 1989.

The AEMS project developed a multicultural ideology fused with an anti-racist stance. Multiculturalism and anti-racism were seen as two sides of the same coin and to work simultaneously. This was not seen as the province of only the arts, but was required to permeate the whole curriculum content and delivery. AEMS was not directly concerned with challenging attitudes but with changing and improving educational practice which can be monitored and evaluated.

Teachers working with AEMS had a framework within which to identify and answer their needs. It was the artists who acted as catalysts of change. Each teacher received in-service provision in the classroom/studio, along with a recommended six days per term for planning and research to acquire new curriculum content associated with the practice of the arts. The work did not only rely on the occasional workshop with a black artist to improve race relations, but also on a systematic approach to ensure effective practice.

The evolution of practice has generally occurred in three phases:

Assimilation

This mirrors the 'colour-blind' approach in education. Arts work tends to be ethnocentric in content with little recognition of students' diversity and the contributions they can make. Students are encouraged to 'correct' their language; practice reflects a cultural deficit approach in which 'ethnic minority' students are seen as culturally deficient and therefore in need of remedial education.

Integration

Responding to initiatives for mutual tolerance and cultural pluralism, provision is made for students to legitimise their own identities: for example, 'West Indian' students are expected to play steel pans and be knowledgeable of the language, cultures and history of the Caribbean. Practice often focuses on one culture, leading to 'tokenism'.

Multiculturalism

Recognition that all cultures are different and have a positive place in the curriculum. Artists work, through the arts, to challenge perceptions and practice.

Antiracism

A realisation that not only must the arts education curriculum be fully multicultural but also that the 'hidden' barriers of attitude and prejudice in the minds of *all* participants be challenged in order to ensure that all pupils can maximise there talents and opportunities through the arts.

Selection of Partners

The Directors of AEMS suggested that partners should be drawn from rural and urban areas with varying levels of multicultural and mono-cultural catchments. Knowing that the Inner London Education Authority was to be dissolved, only one London partnership, Newham was targeted — for a particular 'pin point' project for three terms. Coinciding with the abolition of metropolitan authorities, AEMS, sadly, had no presence in the larger metropolitan regions of the country.

AEMS projects

The Directors of AEMS contacted 160 LEAs in England, Scotland and Wales to identify good multicultural practice and potential partners to extend multicultural arts education.

Letters were sent to schools and colleges, who then dealt directly with AEMS, giving details of their ethnic composition, the extent of multicultural curriculum development and their whole school policy. The first partnership areas established were South Glamorgan, Cheshire, Berkshire, Kingston upon Thames, Kirklees and Walsall. South Glamorgan involved four schools whilst Cheshire was ultimately to involve 36 schools. By early 1989 Newham and Staffordshire had also affiliated to AEMS.

The AEMS Directors recommended chosen LEAs for partnership to the National Committee. A commitment to the Development Plan and a funding contract by authorities and the then Regional Arts Associations were essential criteria for selection.

A co-ordinator was appointed in each of the first six areas; the LEA provided a budget for INSET, for artists and co-ordinators' salaries and overheads. Finance was matched by the Regional Arts Association which was expected to send a representative to the local steering group and support local artists.

During the Spring of 1987, AEMS identified Caribbean, African, South East Asian, Latin American, Chinese and Japanese artists interested in working in education. Between April and September 1987 visual artists, writers, poets and musicians attended AEMS courses to prepare them for projects in schools and colleges. In 1988 and 1989 artists' training included sessions on the implications of the 1988 Educational Reform Act, the National Curriculum and successful models of good practice.

The aims of the artists' training were to focus on children's needs; to develop classroom work and support networks; and to bring skills, knowledge and resources to generally reinforce work in the arts in schools.

INSET days introduced artists to teachers in order to explore methods of collaboration and to increase mutual awareness of forms and processes of artistic expression from a range of cultures. Artists and committee members contributed to conferences, residencies and launch events of regional partnerships.

At the beginning of the project, AEMS directors identified two experienced anti-racist trainers to deliver a two-day courses in each partnership area. The courses developed a understanding of both institutional racism and the barriers to equal opportunities.

Evaluation

At the first meeting of the National Committee on 21 October 1987, there was unanimous agreement that evaluation of AEMS was of vital importance. It was agreed that evaluation exercises should exemplify change — in the ways teachers teach, in administration and in the impact on policy makers. The committee suggested that co-ordinators should gather responses from participating schools and colleges, which would be analysed periodically by the central team in London.

A preliminary review was conducted during the summer term of 1989 by the AEMS Director and Jim Jamieson, a former INSET evaluator of Kingston schools. They evaluated the curriculum achievements of regional groups, assessed the range and quantity of artefacts and assessed the impact of AEMS on teachers and students and used this early evidence to refine and further develop the project. (By this time, AEMS comprised eight regional groups, with combined financial support of £289,460 from education authorities and Regional Arts Associations.)

In the Spring of 1989, Cheshire Education Authority commissioned an evaluation (unpublished) led by David Hustler, to identify perceptions, expectations and roles within the Cheshire AEMS project. Hustler made perceptive observations about organisational politics within the authority, assessing potential barriers and opportunities for Cheshire. Some of the information from this report is incorporated in Chapter Three.

The Model of School and Artist Collaboration

AEMS established a model for effective collaboration between teachers, artists and students. The AEMS director summarised the anticipated procedures:

1. teachers identify broad areas of work.

2. a meeting arranged for teachers to consult with a co-ordinator.

3. coordinator consults with the AEMS central team and researches lists of artists able to match the needs and expertise required.

4. teachers visit the artists at work, in performances at exhibitions, readings or museums.

5. a meeting of the teachers and artists when artists will usually give an account of their approaches and content. There is no obligation on either side but artists are paid for their time.

6. co-ordinator administrates the project organising fees, timescale, materials needed, general co-ordination.

7. teachers liase with the artists, usually at a further meeting, to consolidate plans and prepare students.

8. artists visit teaching venue to observe students at work, meet other teachers and note what resources are available.

9. co-ordinator stands by for unexpected contingencies and plans for review sessions.

10. teacher and students document the work as it takes place.

11. coordinator leads a de-briefing for all involved as part of the evaluation.

12. co-ordinator oversees a follow-up plan designed and undertaken by the teachers.

The main variables noted both in the interim review and the Cheshire evaluation, were:

1. differing roles of the AEMS project in different local curriculum developments.

2. varying status and authority of AEMS teachers.

3. differing flexibility in timetabling between different schools.

4. the variations in awareness of the distinctive features of the AEMS approach and its difference from mainstream arts approaches.

5. the degree of commitment and support from teachers in the same school.

6. the level of support given by Regional Steering Groups.

7. the extent to which monitoring and evaluation depended on the level of resourcing.

8. the length of project ranging between short term 'hit and run' involvement or intensive two to three term projects.

9. the ability to fully incorporate AEMS approaches into ongoing curricula.

Chapter Three

AEMS IN THE SCHOOLS

This chapter presents case study reports from three of the school groups in which AEMS was based. In each the material is largely derived from the reports of participants.

1. SOUTH GLAMORGAN

South Glamorgan, the third largest education authority in Wales, held conferences during 1986 to discuss the implications of the Swann Report. During 1987, the authority sponsored a three-year Education Support Grant (ESG) funded programme to enhance teachers' understanding of the background and experience of ethnic minorities. It had also established a multicultural resources centre, directed by Lois Cox and funded by the Welsh Office.

In the winter term of 1987, AEMS met with South Glamorgan's Assistant Head of Education, head teachers and inspectors. They responded positively to the invitation to join the project, but could not finance the part-time coordinator and teaching cover for planning meetings and training. The problem was temporarily resolved by the AEMS co-ordinating duties being absorbed into the job of Lois Cox at the Resources Centre. From September 1988, the LEA officially allocated two of her five days for AEMS development work. Lois recruited and trained Saeeda Khan, a Welsh Punjabi speaker, to assist with AEMS work. Lois forged together a regional group of teachers representing two primary and two comprehensive schools. Several months later, after the initial AEMS training, two Welsh schools became affiliated members.

It was not until November 1989 that a recognisable steering group, comprising of headteachers and representatives of Commission for Racial Equality, the then Regional Arts Association and LEAs met to discuss the appointment of Lois' successor.

The group's ideal outcomes for the project included:

☐ encouraging holistic approaches to processes;

☐ influencing whole school policy and expanding the curriculum;

☐ recognising that cultural diversity is exciting;

☐ putting children in touch with local and national artists and to exploit local and national resources;

☐ increasing tolerance and respect in society.

The LEA allocated £4850 for each of two years starting in September 1988 conditional obtaining matching funds from the Welsh Arts Council.

The Welsh Arts Council Response

The Welsh Arts Council displayed 'some reticence' after two cordial and seemingly positive meetings with AEMS directors. The Director presented the Development Plan, explaining the financial commitment, and was assured that the Plan would be discussed between both the Council and the the Regional Arts Association (SEWAA). The WAC also advised AEMS at which meetings their application was likely to be considered. There was the expectation that the Welsh Arts Council would provide £12,500 over two years.

Unlike the London based Arts Council, the Welsh Arts Council had no education or ethnic arts sub-committees. It enjoyed autonomy, and its Regional Arts Association structures operated very differently from those of England.

By May 1988, the WAC had twice deferred decision on the AEMS application, stating that the Council's money had been committed without consultation. Members of the local educational and Black communities saw the rejection as evidence of a lack of commitment to multicultural education and Black artists. A campaign of lobbying of the Welsh Office, the Secretary General of the Arts Council, the head of the Office of Arts and Libraries, and the Gulbenkian Foundation urged that the WAC be brought to account for their inaction.

In a letter to Mr C Harnett, then chairman of the Home Office Panel on Race Relations, the Welsh Arts Council wrote 'AEMS raises complex questions and (we) regret the lack of decision on their draft application'.

AEMS was eventually to receive £13,000 over two years from the WAC. Unable to administer the grant themselves, the Council paid the central AEMS office, and delegated a supervisory role to the director of SEWAA. SEWAA had already given steady support to other multicultural projects of the region notably, Theatre Taliesin and the Chapter Arts Centre in Cardiff which had hosted African and Afro-American Dance, Chinese, Asian and Afro-Caribbean theatre.

SEWAA had begun to identify 'the complex questions' stimulated by the AEMS application. The Director and staff had been aware of the issue of multiculturalism. They recognised Wales' position as a nation dominated by the English and fighting to preserve its own language and heritage. There was also awareness of this position being open to charges of nationalism and racism. SEWAA saw the need to maintain the rich traditions of Wales: Eisteddfodau, folk music and dance, a strong amateur tradition in music and drama and a high degree of local participation, with positive responses to the 'new' multicultural Welsh presence.

The Work in Schools: June 1988-September 1989

As the tri-partite funding arrangements settled, teachers of the first four AEMS schools attended three days of training between June and November.

In her progress report, Lois Cox wrote:

> The two parts of the project became more apparent: namely the introduction of skilled, trained Black artists into schools and the underlying implication of such a move which hopefully might foster healthy attitudes in terms of racial awareness and response.

Participants described the anti-racist training as 'inspirational'; the group hoped the training would be taken up by head teachers and deputies from their own and new AEMS schools.

School Projects

The planning process between teacher, coordinator and artist, suggested by the central AEMS office was used to establish AEMS work in Wales.

At first storytelling, batik and puppetry were presented in South Glamorgan schools. The model of relating artists' visits to organised programmes was employed throughout; thus Theatre Taliesin constructed a theatre project around electricity for the science curriculum. Monitoring and evaluation was intended to be conducted by teachers. Lois Cox sent descriptive reports to the London office:

> The school met its first Black artist on November 23 and 24. This was Madge Spencer, a West Indian potter with exceptional communicative skills, who carried out two consecutive morning workshops followed by afternoon sessions where, dressed in Jamaican National costume she told stories, taught games and songs and two dances, as well as introducing artefacts from the Caribbean which children could discuss and handle. This artist's work was of a very high calibre; a *tour-de-force* performance.

The decoration of a secondary school library was the aim of another AEMS craft project. Nina Edge introduced Batik, shisha embroidery, woodwork, stencilling, Islamic design and examples of printing and illustration to stimulate ideas. Examples of this work were later exhibited in the National Exhibition. The group process used by the artists was later used by arts teachers who also utilised African and South Asian images in GCSE art work.

The AEMS group acted as a catalyst for new ways of working and new developments arising out of school-based interests and activities.

October 1989-June 1991

The success of the project and increasing demands on her time led to the coordinator's resignation and by September 1989 the South Glamorgan Education Authority was able to fund a coordinator's post. Nina Edge, a Black visual artist was appointed. Nina had wide national experience, and brought to her new job an awareness of the direct effects of racism on children and young black artists in the Cardiff area. She developed a new role as training provider and identified young, less experienced artists to 'shadow' AEMS employed artists to increase their education skills. Nina observed that Cardiff Black artists were alienated and sometimes forced to leave the locality to develop their art. AEMS thus took on a special significance in developing black artists skills, increasing role models in schools and communities, and offering models to the education and arts authorities.

AEMS work continued in textiles, painting, ceramics, photography, drama and South Asian and Afro-Caribbean music during the next two years. The summer of 1990 saw an ambitious carnival project drawing together dance, design, music and craft skills for a secondary school.

At one of the Welsh primary schools, AEMS established a tri-lingual puppetry project, based on the legend of Gerald of Wales. Conceived in Punjabi, Welsh and English, the final drama piece represented a unique experiment in language development, and an unusual attempt to use language and cultural connections to expand the meaning of a story. The headteacher was impressed with the quality of the artists and the inventiveness of the children involved. The project was later repeated in two other non-Welsh primary schools with similar success. Poetry and prose was the focus of a second bi-lingual project where AEMS brought Welsh and an Afro-Caribbean poets together.

Rhona Choudhury and Vishram Varsani, two Cardiff based musicians, offered South Asian Music and arts work based on Rangoli and Mehendi patterns and colours to two primary schools in response to requests from teachers of design and technology.

Nina Edge, reviewing the AEMS projects reported:

☐ **Music/Dance/Fabric Dyeing**

In conversation — both teaching staff and head teacher agreed that the workshops were a valuable experience, and that some pupils showed a considerable concentration surprising their teachers. This work formed part of the current school project on 'patterns'.

17

☐ **Batik**

Mr Y, head of Visual Arts has commented that for the first time in the memory of the school three Black female students have opted to study Art for 'A' level. Possibly the result of a role model in the classroom.

☐ **Textile Weaving**

The project was reported as a success. The two artists were asked to develop the start already made in the field of textiles. Working with woven textiles in completely contrasting ways, the artists engaged all involved, even those who felt they were 'no good at art' because they lacked drawing skills.

☐ **Music/Dance**

In conversation, a good report back, comments being made that 'even third year boys had danced — and a certain amount of surprise of the rhythmic abilities of all students.

Policy Outcomes for the LEA

Whilst the overall reception of AEMS in Wales was good, the Assistant Director of Education was aware of it frailty. The project was not steered by a group of advisers nor integrated into joint Arts Association and education/arts initiatives. However, two significant developments took place. Due to restructuring within the Authority and a changing awareness of equality amongst its members, a new appointment of a Primary Adviser with specific responsibilities towards equal opportunities was made. The LEA also established a Race Equality Working Party comprising of councillors and members of the Council for Racial Equality.

For the first time within the Authority, a group was formed to tackle issues brought up by advisers or headteachers. The preparation of a report on the extent of incidents of racial harassment and how they had been monitored in schools was cited as an example of the type of work which followed on from the earlier initiatives on multicultural and anti-racist policies.

The restructuring of the Authority presented an opportunity for AEMS to introduce its achievements to new personnel and to raise the issue of greater institutional support for the project.

Policy Outcomes for the Arts Association

Stimulated by the work of AEMS, South East Wales Arts Association continued multicultural arts programmes in additional schools. The Black dance company IRIE was running 64 workshops throughout Wales in the Spring of 1992. The Arts Association was also hoping to find funds for a steel pan tutor with the Cardiff Bay Development Corporation, a project identified some years ago by schools in the area. Longer term plans for multicultural arts depended on the outcome of the plans to establish an integrated system comprising a national Arts Council and locally controlled Regional Boards. The Proposals for the new structure stated that education and equal opportunity policies will be better served by the new structure.

Conclusions

The existence of a national AEMS, with a network of regional co-ordinators, support and resources from the London office, and the authority of a project based in the Arts Council, was fundamental to the success of AEMS in South Glamorgan. There were many strengths of the project, which could not have developed at a purely local level detached from national priorities, resources and expertise. This level of support must be taken into account in development plans for the future.

Strengths

☐ Despite early problems, the Welsh AEMS provided models of arts curriculum development in Welsh and English language schools. The bi- and tri-lingual arts projects were unique and formed ideal ways of expanding the meaning of multiculturalism and helping Welsh students and teachers gained new perspectives of cultural heritages and contemporary problems. Art teachers still working in AEMS schools commented favourably on their experiences of both AEMS INSET and the artists' work in their schools.

☐ AEMS assisted the professional development of a number of Black artists based in Wales and established new partnerships with London based artists.

☐ AEMS projects have stimulated new ways of approaching arts education in schools. Teachers commented that AEMS artists using collective methods of producing work, and validating art and design ideas from non-Welsh home cultures, made them alter their own classroom approach.

19

☐ The success of AEMS artists' visits inspired the then Regional Arts Association to extend multicultural education work with greater confidence than before.

☐ Recognition of the oral, narrative and musical heritage of Wales in designing constructing multicultural arts projects. The skills of research, the potential for bi and tri-lingual development and possibilities for meaningful cultural dialogue are now in place within AEMS Wales, and can be further refined and developed.

Weaknesses

☐ The absence of a Welsh AEMS steering group with authority within the advisory structure meant that, especially in the earlier phase of the project, teachers were steering themselves. This placed great strains on the project, with dependency on only one or two figures in the authority to keep AEMS afloat with personal commitment rather than a strategic management role.

☐ A lack of conceptual clarity surrounding whole school policy development and dissemination of information and practice. The enthusiasm of teachers and artists was not enough to integrate the best of AEMS practice into other areas of the curriculum, nor to extend fully the professional development of teachers.

☐ Documentation and objective evaluation of the work has been weak. Personnel within the LEA or from the community, with wider 'regional' perspectives may have helped teachers realise the value of AEMS work for the future, or assisted them in monitoring and evaluation.

☐ Whilst art advisers were kept fully informed of AEMS work, they had no responsibility within it; neither were they able to take up innovations. Multicultural art work was thus marginalised within the Authority.

☐ The struggle to establish a pool of suitable Black artists for AEMS work showed that artists need much support and encouragement to build their confidence before they can work effectively as catalysts and so stimulate change.

2. WALSALL

This account of the work of the AEMS Project in Walsall is wholly taken from the report produced by Alison Hughes (1992) with permission.

The Organisation of AEMS in Walsall

It was decided that the most effective way of piloting AEMS in Walsall was to work with a small number of schools very closely in order to establish good practice. Initially five schools were selected by the AEMS Management group using criteria of geographical location, past record of multicultural/anti-racist work and ethnic make-up of the school. It was hoped to reflect a range of types of schools in the project. New schools were taken into the project each subsequent year. Each school was asked to select two contact teachers who would attend centrally held in-service training and coordinate and disseminate the project in their own school.

As AEMS progressed more schools expressed an interest in the project and AEMS was able to offer support and training to these schools, so extending the pilot to include 'associate' schools.

The contact teachers attended courses and meetings at Aldridge Court Art and Design Centre, before returning to school to devise a programme of artist's visits. The courses included Racism Awareness which was seen vital to the theoretical underpinning of the project and a series of workshops run by practising black artists to explore the ways in which they could work with children.

The artists' visits were subsequently planned by teachers, artists and the coordinator. They were seen not only as enriching the children's experiences, but also as training for teachers. Artists' residencies were aimed at extending the work that schools already do and, most importantly, they attempted to leave behind a legacy which the schools could develop later.

The Planning of Workshops

One of the basic principles of AEMS is that thorough planning is vital to ensure that the artists' visits are effective. Methods used included:

☐ The artist visits the school prior to workshops and meets the teachers involved. The two parties and the coordinator discuss the proposed projects and agree on a working idea. At the time of this meeting the teachers should know what they ultimately hope to achieve from the work, but should allow the artist to have an input into the planning process. Artists must be paid for their time to attend these meetings and the cost should be part of the initial budget for the project. If the school does not consider an artist suitable after this planning session, they may elect to meet other artists rather than continue. Equally the artist must be happy with the particular school. The coordinator plays a vital role in matching artist and school and negotiating between the two.

☐ The school meets with the coordinator to discuss the type of project/work required. The coordinator then negotiates with artist on behalf of the school. This is not ideal, since the artist's skills are helpful in the planning process. However, if the artist offers a set performance/method of working it is possible to organise visits in this way.

☐ The artist and teacher speak on the telephone. This is not a good planning method, but is possible.

☐ No planning. This is not recommended, but is acceptable in certain cases — for example, performances by theatre companies. In this instance the company should offer good packages of preparation and follow-up work for the teacher to develop.

☐ Teacher sees the artist work in another school or on an in-service course and 'books' the artist to do the same work in their own school.

Curriculum Planning

The following responses were from teachers when asked about how their involvement with AEMS had influenced their planning.

AEMS has given teachers a wider range of knowledge with experience of new materials, resources and starting points and are able to incorporate new approaches into the curriculum.

AEMS has helped schools to develop multi-cultural approaches and enhanced the provision they were making.

Teaching methods have been questioned and more thoughtful approaches have been developed.

AEMS has assisted cross-curricular initiatives. Pressure has been put on administrators to make these initiatives part of the timetable.

AEMS has focused attention and put multicultural education on the agenda of future curriculum development and given multicultural work a high profile.

Teachers have considered issues such as role play in storytelling, co-operative teaching, active styles of learning and the exploration of issues pertaining to morality and social acceptance.

When planning, teachers can draw on a greater awareness in approach and be more able to convey the ideas of a pluralist society.

Teachers are taking cultural diversity into account and not reinforcing sexual or cultural stereotypes.

AEMS has drawn teachers together for planning and developed team work.

From an equal opportunities point of view awareness has been raised about language and illustrations used in school. Documents produced are questioned and altered if need be.

AEMS has given teachers more confidence in planning a wider curriculum and made them more adventurous; 'It pushed my thinking on.'.

AEMS put useful external pressures on the school as a whole and encouraged the development of individual members of staff.

Impact on Learning

The following observations were made by teachers when asked about what felt their students had gained from working with artists.

Skills/Knowledge

Students have acquired new skills, such as kite making and African drum rhythm and the opportunity to handle new materials.

Students have acquired new knowledge including a heightened perception of aspects of other cultures, and an appreciation that there are not just differences between cultures but also similarities and meeting points. They have a developing knowledge of the relationship between Britain and other countries.

Students have been given the opportunity to record how they think and feel about issues through their art along with freedom in expressing their ideas.

Students have benefited from concentrating for long periods on one topic.

Children and young people have produced high quality work. Their work was exhibited, locally and nationally, and they even watched themselves on television!

Experiences and Awareness Raising

The benefits of positive black role models.

White children have been given an insight into what it is like to be black in a white society.

Black children have developed greater self-esteem.

Students have greater understanding of and respect for, values of others with greater awareness of the dangers of stereotyping and an acceptance that it is wrong to generalise about people. They have had personal experience of Black people who have valuable skills which they are competent to share, and who do not fulfil 'popular' images of black people.

Students have opinions and experiences which are of value and can be expressed in a creative way. The importance of a personal expression of feelings has been stressed.

Students from ethnic minorities are more willing to bring their own/family culture into the classroom and not constantly trying to conform to what they perceive as 'white culture'. They have a greater self image and pride in their own culture.

Many children who took part in projects gained in confidence. There was a loss of original self-consciousness, for example boys valued and enjoyed dance.

Co-operation and team work was developed as students worked with artists. Children experienced teachers becoming part of their team and sharing the learning experience. Students were able to work alongside community groups and parents.

Students worked in new ways, for example collaborating in groups or working on large scale projects.

Policy into Practice

Schools' anti-racist and equal opportunities policies were in evidence and could be seen to be working.

Issues of Racism were addressed and there is some appreciation of what racism means.

Enjoyment

Students found that they had enjoyed learning!

Challenges

Teachers made the following responses when asked about problems which could be avoided by other teachers planning projects with artists.

Performance or finished work did not always reflect the standard and depth of the process. The question of process versus product is one which should be considered before the project begins.

Teachers were not always sure how to follow up work done by the artist. Teacher training time should be allocated to each project, and there should be time for teacher and artist to discuss follow-up.

Occasionally projects have been too ambitious — planning needs to be far thinking but also realistic.

Schools sometimes tried to 'spread the artist too thinly' across the school, or work with large classes in an attempt to give the experience to a larger number of pupils. When resources are limited such mistakes are understandable, but experience has shown that a sustained project with fewer children is preferable.

Occasionally artists and schools found relationships with each other difficult to form. This problem is impossible to avoid completely, since an artist who is excellent in one school can be mediocre in another. It is important for teachers to attempt to match an artist to their own requirements rather than duplicate projects which other schools have done.

25

Teachers have sometimes criticised the input of the artist. This is clearly a problem of communication, and teachers need to be clear about objectives when planning with the artist.

Time allocation, in some cases is an important consideration, since development of work has been hampered by too short a time with the artist.

Practical problems such as artists' travel arrangements causing delays, finding appropriate materials and artefacts, mess left after practical session etc. cannot be completely avoided by should be considered in the planning.

The Artists' Comments

Artists have occasionally made criticisms of projects. These include the following points, which can usually be solved at the planning stage:

Problems with payment. This is a major consideration for artists who are working on a free-lance basis and need to be sure that fees will be paid. Artists have sometimes had to wait for several months while the school and authority sort out payment. To solve this problem consideration should be given to how the money can be released to the artist as quickly as possible after the work has been completed.

Artists have arrived to begin a project to find the materials which the school agreed to provide are inadequate for the work.

Occasionally artists have not felt that the school has been welcoming of appreciative of their efforts. It is important for the school to arrange for senior staff to visit the artist at work and also that arrangements are made for food and drink to be provided.

A few artist have experienced racist comments by children. The school must deal with these according to their policy and tell the artist what has been done.

Schools much not use the artists as supply teachers and leave them alone with classes. Apart from the legal implications of this, the project will suffer if artist and teacher do not work as a partnership. Most artists are not qualified teachers and it is the teacher's responsibility to deal with discipline and classroom management.

Major Successes

Teachers were asked not to list specific projects, but to speak generally about the benefits of their AEMS work. They were also asked about any unplanned outcomes.

Publicity gained from projects is most welcome at a time when schools are marketing themselves.

Moving the arts and multicultural education into a high profile in the school.

Raising the spirits of staff and pupils at a difficult time.

Improved communication between staff and the development of a relaxed discussion-oriented approach to work. Closer liaison between staff has been developed.

Enjoyment!

Development of a multi-discipline approach.

The positive reaction and enthusiasm from pupils, teachers and parents.

Teachers were pleased with their personal and professional development. Staff were able to negotiate their own in-service training and receive this alongside their pupils. This cut out the worry, especially for teachers of very young children, of leaving their classes to attend courses. It is also cost effective since supply cover is not necessary.

Children and teachers were extremely proud of the product and displays/ productions improved.

The self esteem of children, particularly black children was improved. The whole school benefited from the presence of black role models. When a group of children in a predominantly black school were told they would be doing Indian kite making their expectations were of a white person making Indian kites. They were delighted to find that the kite maker was Indian!

One project helped a group of pupils with no apparent respect for each other to 'gel' together as a group.

Opportunity for contacts with teachers from other schools on a regular basis.

Friendships have been formed! (One artist was still writing to some of the students met, twelve months after the completion of a project.)

Parents were encouraged to be involved. This was particularly noted by teachers trying to encourage the parents of Asian children to feel welcome in school.

The project had some success in enthusing teachers who are reluctant to be involved in the arts. AEMS co-ordinating teachers and arts post holders were able to use artists' visits to 'enthuse the unenthusiastic'.

Source

Hughes, A (1992) *Arts Education for a Multicultural Society: Walsall*, Walsall: Metropolitan Borough Council Further information from 01922 723687

3. CHESHIRE

This was the largest partnership group of AEMS; its geographical boundary spreading from Manchester in the North, Crewe in the South, Liverpool in the West and Derbyshire in the East. Of its 80 secondary and 500 primary schools, 83 responded to invitations to become AEMS schools.

Initial meetings with the Education Authority led to confirmation of the partnership in March 1988. The Authority had adopted a multicultural statement in 1983 and AEMS was welcomed as a new phase in multicultural strategy.

It was felt that AEMS would also build upon the achievements of language and literacy projects; there was also comment on the 'reasonable' approach of AEMS which, whilst drawing multicultural and anti-racist education themes together, was without confrontation. The strongest support for the project came from advisers in Art, English, Drama, Media Studies, Music and Primary Education. The multicultural advisers, while invited to participate on the steering committee, remained at a distance from the project.

The AEMS partnership programme began in September 1988 with funding procured from the County Council, North West Arts, Merseyside Arts and the Arts Council. The partnership provided funds of almost £90,000 over the four years matched by similar funding by the national project. An advisory teacher in English, with previous experience of the Arts in Schools residencies was seconded to coordinate the AEMS work.

AEMS IN THE SCHOOLS

Representation on the AEMS steering committee comprised of art advisers, primary advisers and Arts Association officers. In common with other partnership steering groups, their first objective was to translate the AEMS Development Plan into local AEMS programme. The committee considered applications from schools and suggestions on AEMS designated teachers. AEMS officers suggested that a balance between rural, urban, white and multicultural schools, prosperous and less affluent schools.

Of the 83 schools which responded to the invitation to join AEMS sixteen schools across the six districts of the Authority were selected according to three criteria:

- [ ] a positive attitude toward multicultural education;
- [ ] the skills and abilities of teachers;
- [ ] position within local clusters.

Phase 1 Programme 1988-90

The AEMS Director suggested a range of artists who might match the curriculum needs being expressed by the schools. At the same time, a programme of INSET training and the Cheshire Launch were planned.

The Cheshire AEMS coordinator consulted with the schools and one college of further education, each with varying experiences of multicultural arts education. The AEMS Steering Group had suggested that each district develop an arts specialism such as drama, media, dance. However consultations with teachers and AEMS artists themselves led to the exploration of cross art themes. Teachers were also assisted in discussion by the AEMS Music specialist (an ethnomusicologist) and the Directors of AEMS.

One of the groups were asked what they thought could be offered by AEMS; the reply was:

- [ ] To teach respect for other races and cultures;
- [ ] To create awareness of other cultures within their own environment;
- [ ] To develop teachers' own knowledge and experience;
- [ ] To destroy insularity.

Whilst the schools of almost all areas were predominantly white, there had been efforts to explore multicultural dimensions through literature, drama and the multi-faith curriculum. There was awareness in at least three schools of racist attitudes amongst children and the catalytic effect that AEMS work might have. The Cheshire coordinator was aware of the need to provide support for teachers and to disseminate examples of good practice.

Schools and Artists

Contrasting with previous Cheshire residencies of poets and writers, AEMS schools hosted sculptors, carnival designers, African-Caribbean musicians, Indian dancers, storytellers and Black writers. During discussion on a Teachers' Day in 1989, participants recognised a range of new skills gained in the arts, their increased confidence in raising issues of race in the classroom and an increasing knowledge of multicultural resources.

Methods of Evaluation

The Cheshire coordinator established a clear process of joint curriculum planning with artists, agreeing national curriculum objectives and developing teaching abilities in the school. Responses of teachers and children were collated in evaluation documents encouraging teachers to assess objectively the impact of the AEMS work. Artists also completed evaluation forms.

Some evaluations illustrating the quality of Cheshire AEMS work were:

Emanuel Jegede — Sculptor, Poet
Primary School Residency: Age 9-11 pupils created a large scale relief painting.

> The aim of the artist's session was to extend the children's' use of their own imagination, so that their approach to clay modelling, drawing, making designs with paper and colour and writing poetry was much broader — as in the African tradition, but not so evident in European approaches.

Emanuel introduced the notions of the artist's 'third eye', his definition of art as an act or creation that is invested with feeling and also arouses feeling, and the fact that every individual is an artist.

The artist told a story whilst modelling in clay. He then built up sand pictures from sand, paint and glue, transferring 'shapes' onto the designs and picking them out in wool relief.

For the art teacher it was:

> ... a most exciting project and stretched the children in many ways:
>
> ☐ understanding Emanuel's philosophy of art;
>
> ☐ finding new meanings for the phrase 'telling a story';
>
> ☐ working with abstract ideas to achieve balance in colour and design;
>
> ☐ working on a very large scale;
>
> ☐ working in a restricted space — it was a challenge for us all to try to get the best use of limited classroom resources;
>
> ☐ team work — considerable organisation was required of each team in order to complete the large scale designs in the time available......
>
> The whole school was intrigued by the transformation of the room each day — I think everyone has a deeper insight into art as a result. Emanuel gave the staff much to think about in his discussions after school about art, craft, mass production of artefacts, authentic African designs and forgeries.....

The artist was correct to state, on his evaluation form, that his work 'contributed to the teacher's aesthetic education and understanding of the link between story telling and visual arts. The artist was also delighted by 'the serious involvement of the children and their reflection of joy and dedication'.

Menai Residential Course

The 5-day AEMS Menai course enabled schools across the county to make contact and creatively engage with AEMS artists. Pupils and teachers from 14 schools, aged 10-13 years worked intensively with artists in sessions of dance, music, literature, visual arts, media and drama. The course aimed to 'extend the artistic skills of the children taking part, to promote racial awareness and to enhance the children's understanding of the art forms of other cultures'. All groups contained a variety of ages and backgrounds; the residential context was both an experience of communal living and sharing, and learning through the arts of diverse cultures. Children from wide ranging social backgrounds, and children with special needs collectively explored their own identities through multicultural learning. For some children, this course was their first experience away from home, in another part of the country. Teachers gained encouragement and support from each other and exchanged ideas. Pupils enjoyed the absence of time restrictions and the opportunity to perform and observe work of the other groups.

By December 1989, the first phase had been completed. The Cheshire project had developed links with internationally renowned artists in London and the North West; more than 100 artist visits had taken place. Schools had increased links across Cheshire neighbourhoods and neighbouring counties. As enthusiasm increased to continue the project, the AEMS steering committee commissioned an evaluation report in the hope of mustering further political support and finance.

The Cheshire Evaluation

The Evaluation team from Didsbury College of Education and Crewe and Alsager College (now both constitute parts of Manchester Metropolitan University) presented their report in April 1990.

The team conducted 30 interviews with AEMS co-ordinators, artists, teachers, headteachers, advisers and group discussions with children in workshops. Their objectives were to focus upon models of good practice and to point to factors affecting development of the project. Their research coincided with early pilots of the National Curriculum. Local Management of Schools and the radical restructuring of advisory and inspector structures were not on the horizon at the time. The report celebrates the ambitious nature of Cheshire AEMS, whilst adding several cautionary conclusions.

Of the AEMS work itself, the evaluators observed:

> the powerful grassroots experiences between artists, pupils and the teachers involved became visible through the ambitious structures set up by the project.

The report states that Cheshire AEMS will be recognised nationally for representing a useful model for multicultural work in a largely white, indigenous population. However, rather than embark upon another phase 'where a hundred flowers may bloom', a next phase was seen to require a different management structure. Researchers noted that a large number of respondent had expressed a form of 'It's been wonderful, but now what?' with real concern, and on occasion, a strong sense of impending loss were the project to be contracted or closed down.

Evaluators felt that more meaningful guidelines on what an AEMS project should be about should be formulated by the LEA and headteachers. The AEMS project was not designed as a team effort; the challenge for future phases lay in extending the commitment to multicultural education beyond the arts advisory group, to involve the advisory management team as a whole.

The key conclusions of the report may be summarised as follows:

1. There is a need for a clearer sense of what multicultural and associated anti-racist policies and practice should look like; the identification of the project as an individual vision must change to one of team identification, with shared responsibilities;

2. AEMS concerns should continue within a broadly based arts development;

3. The role of visiting artists in schools already involved may need to be re-examined; this is related to the observation of the multicultural 'learning continuum' between 'festivals' and 'whole school multi-cultural education';

4. All schools should undertake a curriculum audit and a staff development needs analysis to identify where they are on the continuum and know how to get to their next goal.

5. There should be neither change in key personnel of the project nor change in basic structure of artists' visits;

6. The county must develop multicultural and anti-racist work further to enable staff development of those involved. The management team will need support in the management of innovation and change.

Finally, the evaluation highlighted two areas for further investigation. These were firstly, the means through which the learning experience is enhanced by Black artists, and which activities in schools are most formative. Secondly, an investigation into the nature of teachers' understanding of concepts crucial to success.

The report concluded:

> A useful context-appropriate start has been made at a variety of levels. We also note that the project had engendered, particularly at grassroots level, a considerable and unanticipated amount of goodwill, enthusiasm and commitment.

The report emphasis that the LEA must develop a coherent and planned response to the concerns of impending loss;

> A pessimistic view of the future is that the project will be seen to have not worked after all, because it did not receive necessary strategic attention at senior level at a crucial time. An optimistic view is that Cheshire has the opportunity to realise its potential to develop a powerful approach to Arts Education for a Multicultural Society. In so doing, Cheshire will also enhance and broaden its rich arts tradition. (pp48-9)

Responses to the Evaluation

The positive tone of the evaluation provided the rationale for continued support within the Authority. The key personnel of the project felt that it was a fair appraisal of progress. However the recommendations regarding structure of management, formulation of a new strategy for new and established AEMS schools, areas for further investigation to enhance staff development and understanding of pupil and teacher learning were not heeded. As the demands of the National Curriculum increased, together with increasing instability of LEA structures and the management of schools, it was easier to minimise change, rather than to seize the evaluators' suggestions of innovation.

Project Development 1991-1992

The second phase of the project developed as the first, with a new core of 16 schools and AEMS teachers. By this time, a team of experienced teachers with skills and understanding of new models of multicultural practice had developed. The Cheshire group developed resources in video, literature and showcase exhibition materials. Schools purchased African and Caribbean instruments and art works. The coordinator and those she trained also possessed expertise in negotiating for funds, managing artists' residencies and facilitating partnerships between artists and schools. The engagement of professional artists led to new connections between schools and arts and exhibition venues. Until the AEMS project, only two schools in the region had visited the Commonwealth Institute. The model of country and urban twinning tried by two schools who visited Manchester and Liverpool was clearly successful in terms of cultural and social history education.

Strengths of the Cheshire AEMS

☐ Altered teachers' perception of arts education practice, involvement with artists opened up new curriculum developments which did not exist before.

☐ Offered many catalytic experiences in a 'Festival of Whole School Education' continuum. It has:

— stimulated thought and action on anti-racism;

— highlighted the need for policies and action;

— affirmed the beliefs of schools already committed to multicultural education through whole school education.

☐ Trained at least 64 teachers in new skills, at varying levels across performing arts, literature, oracy and media arts, in ways which can be utilised practically in the classroom.

☐ Engendered a county resource of artefacts such as sculptures, friezes, musical instruments to support the development of multicultural arts education.

☐ Provided a model of multicultural curriculum development appropriate for predominantly white areas, albeit with an economically and socially diverse population.

☐ Created a core of teachers who have taken on 'ambassador' roles in encouraging similar initiatives in other rural or suburban parts of Britain.

☐ Harnessed the resources of its Arts Associations and therefore helped them to demonstrate their commitment to multicultural art development and education.

☐ The accessible increased professional awareness of exhibition and performance venues which can be used as multicultural curriculum resources.

☐ Provided 'powerful grass roots experiences' for many hundreds of children; it has provided and important creative tool for those schools already active in whole school education.

☐ Engendered a model of sharing amongst professional educators in an innovative project with many uncertain outcomes. It has thus opened up possibilities for other curriculum and cross-phase collaborations.

☐ Enhanced the educational skills of many Black and cultural minority artists, extending their abilities to work in a variety of educational context.

☐ Through the residential courses, artists have been able to explore new methods of collaboration across art forms, and using the skills of teachers to improve the educational impact of their work.

Weaknesses

☐ A lack of theoretical underpinning, identified in the first phase by the Steering Committee, and observed by the later independent evaluation.

☐ A lack of integration with other multicultural and equal opportunity initiatives in the Authority; there are few Black role models in the education infrastructure.

☐ Little representation of cultural minority groups, parent associations and governors on the steering committee. The opportunity for widespread dissemination of the work was thus not fully realised.

Chapter Four

AEMS AND FURTHER EDUCATION

As in the previous chapters the information draws heavily on the reports of the participants.

In DES Circular 9/87 which set out the LEA Training Grants Scheme priorities for 1988-89, a new category was added to the list of national priorities: 'Training in the teaching and planning of the FE curriculum in a multi-ethnic society.' Equal opportunities, multicultural education and racial equality were further underlined by the retention of national priority status in 1990-91. The Further Education Unit took forward a range of initiatives embracing course content, staff and student recruitment and college codes of practice.

AEMS worked from January 1989 to December 1990 in the Further Education sector. During this time a range of activities was undertaken including work in the visual and performing arts sections of four colleges, the training of Black artists to work in FE, an in-service weekend and two national seminars.

AEMS enabled colleges to develop multicultural arts curriculum resources, enhance access to Further Education for Black and cultural minority students and explore anti-racist teaching and learning strategies. The AEMS programmes were integral to a comprehensive staff development initiative known as RP390.

Partnerships with Dewsbury College of Further Education, Walsall College of Art, Huddersfield Technical College, Mid-Cheshire College and South Cheshire

College were established to pilot AEMS curriculum materials which linked into BTEC and Vocational Training. Arts advisers, AEMS co-ordinators and education officers selected FE colleges in close proximity to developing AEMS school projects. The more extensive curriculum development programmes at Huddersfield and Dewsbury Colleges are described in the case studies below. Walsall College organised a 4-day residency supported by college visits to 'The Other Story' a major Black art exhibition in London at the time.

The then Further Education Unit of the then Department of Education granted AEMS £10,000 for 1988/89 increasing to £17,500 for 1989/90.

The three art and design case studies illustrate what has been achieved within three colleges who target BTEC level courses. Dewsbury College highlights the need for the right brief and uses the voices of students and artists to explore the project; Walsall College of Art documents the process of using the stimulus of a major Black exhibition; and Huddersfield Technical College identifies recruitment issues and focuses on the essential planning stage.

CASE STUDY 1: Dewsbury College

Dewsbury College serves the Pennine cities of Yorkshire and the towns of Halifax, Dewsbury, Huddersfield and Wakefield. It offers foundation, First and Higher and National Diplomas in art, design and fashion.

The Course

The BTEC National Diploma Photography course attracts students from local areas plus a number of overseas students from France, Iceland and Ireland.

Student aspirations vary from the wish to enter higher education at degree level or higher national level to starting their own business at the end of the course. The BTEC philosophy states that students' training should meet the needs of industry and their education should allow them access to higher level courses. This two year course focuses on the professional role of the photographer within the art and design industry and includes an introduction to the creative and technical aspects of photography.

Usually the brief for this course is based upon a one week timescale. Issued to students on the Friday, work commences on the following Monday with a critique and evaluation on the following Friday. The work normally concludes with students presenting a final set of photographs either in print or transparency form. The type of brief is usually vocationally orientated and reflects the needs and practices of the industry.

The Project

The aim of the project was to assist students in their understanding of the photographer's perception of the persuasive power of images; to increase the understanding of professional practices; and develop the individual in professional, practical, social and life skills. The project lasted for eight weeks.

The lead staff member decided that, as none of the existing briefs could retain their initial aims and objectives and satisfy the multicultural nature of the AEMS initiative, a new set of briefs had to be written.

The Briefs
The Identity Crisis

There are many people who are descendants of immigrants to this country. They are born and educated here and live their lives without a thought for 'roots' or the

39

homeland of their parents. Others take on the identity of their parents and impose a 'false' or 'true' nationality upon themselves. It is up to you to investigate and illustrate this area. It is up to you who you illustrate and how you portray this issue.

The Role of Women Within an Ethnic Minority

The modern European woman has travelled a long way along the road to emancipation during the last fifty years. It is not impossible to visualise women doing work of any nature as we approach the year 2000. The religious and cultural values within the ethnic communities have had an effect upon the development of women within their communities. It is your job to visualise and interpret the fundamental differences, if any, between the women of ethnic cultures and indigenous European women.

The Provision of Muslim Schools

There is at the moment a contentious issue regarding the provision and state support of Muslim schools. There has been a long tradition of the Church supporting and providing education within this country. There is not a problem with the raising of capital for these schools, only the state funding is being argued. This has created a rift, posing a major threat to race relations within this country, and especially this area. You are to investigate the consequences of the current difficulties and visualise or portray it from your personal viewpoint.

Students were asked to produce a photo-journalism essay in the form of six final prints accompanied by a short note of explanation. The work, of exhibition standard, was to contribute to a major College exhibition.

Barry Jefferies, the AEMS Co-ordinator for Kirklees, was instrumental in negotiating the project. He offered funding, advice and contacted appropriate people to help Dewsbury College realise its aims. As the planning stage developed, a team of Asian and African-Caribbean practitioners and artists presented their work to the students. This served to place the briefs within a vocational context and began the students' research.

The project leader wrote that 'several of the situations discussed were disturbing to the students involved'. However, the tutorials and the visual and written materials for the briefs illustrated 'the progress made in self development by individuals'.

Students described research and development of their ideas for their projects, and changes in their own perceptions.

Responses to the briefs:
STUDENT A.
The Role of a Muslim Woman
As I started this project, I hadn't a clue what I was doing; I was going into it totally blind. I did a lot of research at the library and visited a lot of people who had contacts with Muslim families. I contacted about 10 families; they all said no. Most of them would have been happy to talk to me, but not let me take photographs. I eventually found Shider, who let me photograph her niece.

I showed Shider my drawn ideas and my comments. I then asked for hers. I then put both our views together and put them under the photograph. Each photograph is about a Muslim woman.

Old and New Values
A comparison of old and new upbringing of western and eastern values. Behind is similar contrasts like a modern television with video and, above, an eastern cloth.

Muslim Women Wear Saris
Muslims women cover their heads to respect people they do not know. This is part of their religion.

A Burka forms a Barrier for Muslim Women
'Burka' is a piece of material which covers most of a woman's body. Men will not look at her when wearing this, so she feels safe; it also forms a barrier.

He is always the Head of the Family
The pyramid shape of saris with the male hat at the top making it look as though the male is the leader of the women.

Muslim Girl Doesn't Understand. No Communication at School
A Muslim girl has drawn a picture for her mother on Mothers' Day. It is of a western woman.

STUDENT B.

The Identity Crisis

In my AEMS work I have tried to take a slightly different approach to tackling the brief. Being Black, I have tried to put more of my own personal experiences into the work. This has resulted in me taking a more abstract visual approach, using photocopies, and my own childhood family photos to add a further sense of personal involvement.

The use of abstract imagery, to illustrate the issues I have chosen to highlight, especially since personal memories and experiences are such a large component of the work, allowed me to make quite complex statements in a concise and concentrated way. A documentary/reportage approach would have made it difficult, if not impossible, to show the kind of specific ideas that I developed for my work.

Adopting this approach, I have tried to use myself and my experiences as the object of scrutiny for the camera, rather than scrutinising other people, as most of the other students have been forced to do.

Accusation

This piece of work was developed from the day to day reality of other people's suspicious and paranoia towards black youths. Accusing looks and reactions that make you feel like a dangerous criminal deviant, with no chance to show the kind of person you really are.

It's almost as if when they look at you they see something different from what you see in the mirror. Almost as if they see some sort of dangerous animal or deranged criminal lunatic. The image attempts to show what people's minds turn us into.

Confusion

The concept behind this piece of work was developed, after hearing the racially inflammatory comments of Norman Tebbit, his so-called 'cricket test speech'. The problem of cultural and social icons is a very serious issue that causes great anguish and confusion to many young ethnic minority children. The desire to see black success, adopt black role models, and see your own aspirations reflected in the success of other black individuals, organisations and institutions can cause a dual conflict and a great sense of confusion. This confusion is what the image is trying to communicate.

Division

'I'm no racist, but it's not right, not you and my daughter.' At some point in life most Black males will have this comment or a similar one levelled at them. However, I don't view this as an issue of over-protective fathers, I see it as a racist manifestation of a basic sexist problem in men. The view expressed seems to me to have a lot more to do with male attitudes about control and possession of females in the family and community that seems to completely ignore women as individual human beings, and views them more as a sexual resource.

STUDENT C.
The Provision of Muslim Schools

One of the things that is hardest to do in photography is to accurately reflect a different culture to one's own. This is why the world is full of stereotypes of what the rest of the world is like.

My brief was to look into the question of state funding of Muslim schools. I needed a guide to help me through the maze of arguments and found a community leader and we talked for many hours on the subject. It was not long before I realised that there were much wider issues at stake than funding alone.

In the Muslim religion education is of prime importance. One of the first lines in the Koran speaks of the importance of education. In the Muslim religion, to have a good education is the most wonderful gift. If only Britain had this attitude towards the subject!

A Muslim school was the focus of my photographs. I wanted to disband myths. In my photos I wanted to concentrate on the more abstract symbols and signs that I felt contained the essence of the school. I wanted to move well away from the conventional way of approaching such a project.

When I entered the school certain things surprised me. A collage of pictures of cars on the wall cut from glossy magazine adverts. A strange irony when hardly any advertising is aimed at the Asian community. One shot that particularly sums up the whole situation is that next door to the Muslim schools is a modem state school. Everything is bright plastic, the playground is full of playthings and the whole place must have cost a fortune...

The project has been a very important learning process and has been a great insight into a different way of life and an important opportunity to question your own values.

AEMS artist input

The course leader invited AEMS artists and the college multicultural officer to lead seminars to provide social and historic background to the subject areas of the brief. The artists, all of whom had considerable experience of AEMS projects, highlighted a range of political and educational issues present in the Dewsbury College experience. One artist wanted to know:

> how far the college went in terms of challenging racist and sexist images if they were to manifest themselves... if we were to challenge students' images because of racist and/or sexist content, how much support would we get?

The visiting artists raised awareness of misrepresentation, visual stereotyping and the particular viewpoint of Asian women photographers. A women only seminar was subsequently held.

The following extracts describe artists' critical perception of the project and illustrate how they guided students towards a new understanding of the issues stimulated by the project.

The writings formed part of the final evaluations, and were supported by a model design brief suggesting a greater integration of communication and art history studies in assignments. Artists' recommendations chiefly concerned institutional support and the strengthening of equal opportunity practice. An AEMS photographer wrote:

> I think the issue of access to photography and equipment, which relates to control and power in our society needed to be addressed. It is predominantly white people who take photographs of Black people and in doing so, reinforce stereotypical images of Black people as 'passive' rather than 'active' beings, while white people are being voyeuristic looking into Black peoples' lives without placing them in the context of overt and covert racism.

Comment

The major comment by the lecturer, students and artists/practitioners was on the type of brief set. The intention was to match the aims of a vocational course with

AEMS philosophy and practice. Existing briefs could have been altered to reflect specific cultures but the lecturer wanted to present a challenge for himself, the students, the College and its courses.

Many of the students had reservations particularly as their normal work pattern had been disrupted. In the early stages many questioned the validity of the project and wanted to know how the experience would make them better photographers.

The practitioners who were sent the brief were anxious because they thought that it would encourage students to use photography in a voyeuristic way and therefore undermine the intentions of the AEMS project. One practitioner stated 'Black cultures are seen as 'problem', as homogeneous, static, and exotic. It neglects social, political and economic power, and sees racism as 'personal', not 'structural'. There is a danger that this approach would reinforce prejudice and stereotypes.'

The briefs were also very open and the eight week process relied on a high degree of student personal choice, realisation of the issues and the ability to assimilate these tensions into a final product. Some students felt that they were being experimented upon for ends which were not clearly stated and to work without a commercial direction was a difficult concept to grasp.

To some extent the students were left to discover or make sense of the issues themselves and this was both a major strength and weakness of the brief.

Outcomes

Many students spoke of their experiences during the project and of how the process had changed their views. One recalled how his mother had hurled racial abuse at a Black woman because she would not move her car. The student took issue with his mother as he could not tolerate the use of 'Black' insults and statements such as 'all Blacks are the same.' He explained that prior to working on the AEMS project he would not have said anything or thought that such comments were offensive.

In terms of self development many of the students demonstrated progress in both perception of the issues and their responsibility as a producer of images. They had not thought that through the camera they could look at themselves as not only mechanics of picture-making but also authors of photographs which were constructed in partnership with those being photographed.

For the College staff discussion focused on issues to do with ethics, integrity, sensitivity, responsibility, and the moral use of images. At a course review meeting it was decided that the:

☐ number of projects would be reduced enabling more time for deeper investigation and research into projects;

☐ projects would be given to small groups to allow for on-going student research so that greater emphasis could be placed upon the identified areas of need

☐ 'The Corner Shop' project would go as it had led to a succession of stereotypical images and caused concern amongst staff who had taught the brief.

☐ tension between working on issues within a short timescale would be eliminated if assignments were integrated. Inputs from other sections would support the main brief and allow a greater immersion within each project.

CASE STUDY 2. Walsall College Of Art

The Course
The BTEC National Diploma General Art and Design is a two year full-time course. The four main areas of study are Fine Art, Graphics, 3-Dimensional Design, and Fashion and Textiles. Students eventually specialise in one area to give them the basis for entry into Higher Education or employment in their chosen field.

The Project
The project began with a visit by a group of first year students to 'The Other Story' exhibition at the Hayward Gallery in London. The project was a collaboration between AEMS and the South Bank Centre. Students were given a gallery tour by an AEMS artist who discussed how the exhibiting artists had represented themselves in relation to culture, race, gender and sexuality.

The aim of the project was to use the exhibition as a stimulus for work back at the College. Students made notes on a number of issues that they would explore later during the practical part of the project. The response to the exhibition was very positive as everyone found something with which they could identify.

The AEMS artist worked for 4 days over three weeks. Students were able to sustain their interest from one week to the next and for some the extra time allowed their ideas to mature.

The first session began with a short slide presentation of some of the artist's work which spanned several years. He discussed his working methods of mixed-media using photography, photocopy, paint and textiles with image and text. The brief arose out of a discussion with the students around different forms of memory and history stimulated by The Other Story exhibition; of how visual language involves a dual activity as well as a whole cultural system which affects the viewing, interpretation and consequently as artists, the production of work. The artist selected themes from the exhibition and in doing so, began to touch on complex issues such as 'culture' and 'identity'. Students were encouraged to think of how they would represent themselves using portraiture in a narrative form.

The Briefs:
Theme of 'Auto-Portraits'
Make notes and collect information about your past and about what was important or influential for you. This will be developed into a visual plan so you will need to find visual means to represent written notes.

Look at the use of language [written and visual] and how you can develop a personal language to explore and communicate the things which are important or particular to you. Consider the use of personal photographs and objects as part of this language.

Look at how other artists have developed their own languages or style.

Create a portrait of yourself looking at the different influences affecting who you are. These could include family, environment, culture [music, fashion, media]. Look at how you remember and interpret the past and how you use the past to understand the present. Explore this through personal memory, family history, cultural and national history.

Look critically at what you are trying to say and how clearly you are saying it.

Responses to the brief
STUDENT A.
'A Rich Man's Heaven is a Poor Man's Hell'
This piece of work is about how some people/nations have far too much money, whilst others have too little. Money doesn't make you a better person.

STUDENT B.
'Body Facism'
Nobody is perfect, but everyone would like to be. Women are always trying to alter their image to fit into the stereotype of the perfect woman. I am one of them; I have tried to show how I am influenced by this as well. Why are we always trying to change ourselves? Why can't fat be beautiful?

STUDENT C.
'Sisters'
This is about my sister and I and how through the years we have become strangers, since she left home.

STUDENT D.
'Me'
This is about 'Me'
About my family
my Idol
my Nations
and my thoughts.
Amen.

STUDENT E.
This piece of work illustrates the relationship between my sister and me, how we have grown apart and almost lost contact with each other.

Comment
For many of the students, the initial response relied on immediate symbolism — hearts for love, light colours for joy, dark colours for sadness, flags for nationality. The ambiguities and problems of such symbolism were discussed. Students were encouraged to explore the use of different media and work in the

most appropriate materials to realise their ideas. They were encouraged to use text in a narrative, poetic form rather than as documentary information.

During the project the students were encouraged to develop a critical attitude towards their own and each others work. At the beginning or end of each day work would be displayed and students would assess it according to how successfully it conveyed the intentioned ideas.

The artist commented: 'Critical visual literacy as well as a general analytical approach to information has to be an integral part of art education. There appears to be an enormous chasm between contemporary art practice and art education in schools. For Black artists there is a pressure to follow an uncritical multicultural approach and produce cultural objects [kites, masks] rather than deal with underlying issues of culture itself.'

Outcomes

As the project developed the students were invited to show their work at Wolverhampton Art Gallery alongside the touring exhibition of 'The Other Story'. This completed a cycle: from visiting an exhibition, to producing work based on ideas which arose from it, to having the work exhibited alongside the original stimulus.

Many students described the project as being decisive and inspirational and mentioned the project in their college applications. The students have also been enthusiastic about researching themes relevant to Equal Opportunities, and have explored subsequent themes such as art and design of other cultures, representations and images of people in the media; advertising and stereotypes and sexuality in art.

During 1990 the Equal Opportunities team at the College of Art were struggling to write a policy. As Chairperson of the Equal Opportunities Group the lead lecturer felt supported and encouraged by the AEMS project. The draft of the Equal Opportunities Policy was completed, and a 'Tea-Party' launch was held, attended by representatives from the community, staff and students.

The small staff team involved in the project felt more enabled to present issues of gender and race as part of their regular curriculum and it was evident, after the

AEMS initiative, that the students had been 'sensitised' and wanted to continue the process.

The College is now involved with the planning of a local Festival of Black Arts in conjunction with the community. This has stemmed from connections with Walsall Youth Arts Project and the Black Sisters Group. Students have also been involved with preparations for the 'Women and Work' exhibition at Walsall Museum.

The AEMS work enabled the staff and students of the College to share both positive and negative experiences which indicated that the institution was accepting the urgency of the need for change.

CASE STUDY 3: Huddersfield Technical College

The Art and Design Department of Huddersfield offers drawing, graphic design, printmaking, photography, fashion/textiles, 3D and media studies from Foundation to Higher National level.

The Course

Research was undertaken by the Art and Design staff in response to the small number of Black and Asian students recruited into Art and Design Courses; disproportionate both to the College generally and the community at large. The staff felt that Highfields, the location of the Art and Design Department, was perceived as an unwelcoming site for Black and Asian students.

As a result of the research, it was proposed that the staff establish and maintain close liaison with schools, community centres and groups, and promote positively the opportunities provided for Art and Design careers offered by the BTEC First Diploma Course.

The First Diploma is a group-based course and broadly covers drawing; graphic design; printmaking; photography; fashion/textiles; 3D and media studies. In addition students undertake a programme of Integrated Studies for one morning a week.

The course is delivered thematically. The first term, for example, will use the theme of 'Architecture' to enhance the interaction and mutually supportive nature of the component disciplines. The final term is devoted entirely to the students' individually chosen and negotiated Major Assignments.

Huddersfield Technical College was invited to participate in the AEMS initiative and the BTEC First Diploma Course in Art and Design was identified because it was flexible and the thematic and student-centred nature of the course delivery involved live projects within the community. The course offered realistic career progression in Art and Design and the staff felt that this would ultimately change the recruitment patterns at the College.

The Project
The original idea for the project was that work would be generated by the interaction of social/cultural groups of young people in and around Huddersfield. The ultimate aim was to host an exhibition which would 'celebrate' the lives of young people in Huddersfield.

Preliminary meetings with AEMS designers and discussions with the students, highlighted the problems of making such a vague notion work. Five artist designers from AEMS discussed how image-grabbing in the local communities would be counter-productive to the major aim of the project. During this time, staff participated in a two day Racism Awareness Training course, to help them form their initial approaches.

The Multicultural Education Co-ordinator of the College arranged a meeting with representatives of local community groups and associations. Through community contacts the College was able to focus on four centres which would offer the students the opportunity to undertake live projects.

Two days were allocated at the end of the planning term for the students to be shown work by the five designers and to discuss the potential involvement with the selected centres. The main focus was for the students and designers to meet and familiarise themselves with each other. The professionalism and expertise of the designers served as a positive role model for the students.

After much research the agreed aims of the project were to

☐ harness the skills of the Art and Design students around projects proposed by local Community Centres;

- □ develop awareness in Highfields staff and students of the issues and problems encountered by local multicultural community groups (eg. marginalism, racism).
- □ provide a basis for a continuing relationship between Highfields and local communities.
- □ promote curriculum development which embraces something more than a Eurocentric approach across all Art and Design courses.

At the start of the spring term work began by introducing the students to staff at the Centres and engaging in dialogue necessary to meet the requirements of the brief. The students met with community representa- tives and focused on the role of the Centres and issues faced by communities and individuals in a multicultural society.

The Brief. Project Title. Celebration

A 13 week project of which the first 4 weeks constitute individual exploration and group research. Students will work in groups on the theme of Huddersfield as a multicultural society.

Client requirements included:

Birkby and Fartown Community Centre — new logo and promotional materials; The Hudawi Centre — promotional graphics for their recording studio and multicultural play clothes for the day nursery; The Indian Workers Association — ceramics, textiles, interior graphics and a model to be used in fund raising for a proposed Sikh Centre; The Pakistan Association — video and photographic images as learning materials for women's English classes.

The term's work led to an exhibition with an accompanying catalogue and edited video, concerned with both process and product.

Supported by Highfields staff, visiting designers worked one day a week with students to implement the brief. The exhibition showed work and explained the process involved and was to be completed to the satisfaction of the Centre involved.

Responses to the brief:

STUDENT A.

At first I thought that this project would be getting our work for nothing and that we would get nothing much out of it. But now I have found we are getting a lot of work out of it and it is interesting because this time we are working for a real client.

STUDENT B.

I didn't know that there was a Sikh religion. I didn't know much about India either. I only knew a little about Hindus and Muslims. When we first started the project I didn't know what was wanted. It was a mix of confusion and bewilderment, but I am glad that the artists came which helped us get into the project.

STUDENT C.

The project has given me the chance to work with artists on a one to one basis, the fact that I was working with Black people has given me a greater awareness of the different cultures in and around Huddersfield. Before I started the project I hadn't worked with or known any Black or Asian people because the school I went to had a very small minority of Black people to whom at the time I didn't pay too much attention.

Outcomes

The exhibition opened as scheduled and the catalogue 'Design for the Community' gave details of designers, staff and student perspectives.

The College now has a model for continuing dialogue with communities. The staff have earned respect from community groups and have shown a commitment to equal opportunities.

The initiative enabled all students to locate their design aptitudes; develop a professional approach to design work; feel confident in the importance of their own cultural heritage; and communicate these strengths effectively in interview. These abilities resulted in 100% placement of students onto their first choice of further design education.

For staff the initiative generated a range of skills which have enabled them to develop to pluralistic Art and Design education; undertake community group liaison; further to equal opportunities in a non-confrontational manners; and undertake staff development and training.

Traditionally the points of entry for pluralistic Art and Design education have been in the context of 'marginal areas' such as supporting and communication studies or through the tutorial system. The AEMS initiative allowed the staff to establish non-eurocentric education at the heart of the design studies programme. Supporting and communication studies now have a pivotal role in establishing that equal opportunities are essential for successful design work.

The primary factor in ensuring the success of the response to the AEMS initiative was the assumption that it marked the beginning of a continuing process. But the contribution by the Black designers to staff development has also been fundamental. Without this input, together with the role models provided by black staff or visiting designers, the continuing process of course review and evaluation would not have been possible.

The AEMS initiative has unlocked an additional £6,500 from the Authority and College for further curriculum development work. Applications have been made for Section 11 funding in order to continue the programme for three years with the aim of establishing the programme as a permanent feature of all mainstream Art and Design work at Huddersfield Technical College.

Curriculum and Institutional Issues

Staff in further education are surrounded by a series of different innovations: the development of national vocational qualifications, the integration of information technology, the extension of work-based learning and assessment. These innovations are often juggled with staff projects and at times there is a tension between team, institutional and government initiatives.

The purposes of any curriculum innovation is to bring about improvement in practice. For those trying to bring about curriculum change for a multicultural society, the work is surrounded by confusion and contention about what is meant by the change, what it should involve, what outcomes might be expected and what policy should exist. Even where managers are working for understanding, where they have objectives, policy and implementation targets, where they have money and have appointed staff, where they support staff development, operate good personnel policies, are committed to improvement, and even where the innovation is seen by them as prestigious in some way, it is likely that there will be difficulties. Here are some which may be recognisable:

Staff are busy, faced with many innovations and pressures, and lack time. Communications may be difficult between people who share an interest in the innovation. There will be conflicts of belief, some of which may not be capable of reconciliation, some of which individuals may not be aware they have. Money is short and innovations compete for it.

There may be a lack of knowledge about what is going on in other areas of the institution and particularly outside, and a lack of empowerment to access such knowledge.

So what kind of strategies can be adopted by staff and managers?

Some questions:

- ☐ What are your own needs? Where are you in terms of your own knowledge?

Do you know, for example,

- ☐ what FE for a multicultural/multi-ethnic society means to you? your students? what should it mean?
- ☐ what the policy is in your institution? the LEA?
- ☐ who was involved in formulating it?
- ☐ what is the implementation plan?
- ☐ what are the targets?
- ☐ the who and what of resourcing?
- ☐ what is involved in evaluation and review?
- ☐ which people are involved?
- ☐ what are their roles?
- ☐ where your work fits in?
- ☐ who are the people in your organisation implementing this change? other changes?

☐ who the people are outside your organisation who have an interest? The LEA, the region, the Training and Enterprise Council? The examining or validating body?

☐ who is-in charge of funding allocations for this area of work?

☐ what your organisation's personnel policy looks like?

Are you able to describe:

☐ what your own 'mini-policy' is?

☐ what you are doing now for this work?

☐ what you have already achieved? what is good and going well?

☐ what is going badly?

☐ what time you are spending on this area of work?

☐ what you can realistically achieve in an identified time span?

Some questions for curriculum planners:

Recruitment

☐ How are courses marketed — what is the ideal target group for the course?

☐ Does current intake reflect this ideal?

☐ What is the ratio of Black students with regard to level of course?

☐ How realistic/viable is progression for Black students from lower to OND level, for example?

☐ What strategies are there to evaluate and remedy any perceived recruitment imbalance?

Implementation

☐ How qualified are staff to implement Equal Opportunities Curriculum Development?

☐ Have staff undertaken Racism Awareness Training?

☐ What proportion of staff (F/T, P/T or visiting lecturer) are Black?

☐ What dialogue exists between Course/Section/Department and local Black communities?

☐ What use is made of such dialogue in devising curriculum content?

☐ Would an amended curriculum meet existing external examining/ validating bodies' requirements?

Development

☐ What strategies are there to embed equal opportunities principles into the mainstream curriculum to avoid the usual 'bolt-on' implications of such initiatives?

☐ How can it be ensured that equal opportunity is given in the recruitment of Black staff?

☐ What support systems (Mentor, Staff Training etc.) can be provided to ensure that such curriculum development be effectively delivered?

☐ How can the issues raised by these questions be given appropriate priority on the College agenda?

Strategies then come into six key areas:

— accepting that support has to be worked for

— finding the time to reflect, think and plan realistically

— getting the knowledge needed, getting the evidence needed

— finding the people needed

    — to reduce isolation and extend contacts and knowledge

    — to access information

    — to support action

    — to provide criticism

— working to clarify beliefs, aims and targets while putting plans into action

— expecting and using failures as opportunities to develop

The dissemination of good practice is much needed to help other colleagues in the field develop discussion and initiate change. However this should not be viewed solely as a personal remit — there is a need for effective support structures to enable all staff to continue developing their work.

Networking may be the best place to start because staff may be able to exchange information, offer advice and support; they may have ideas or it may be possible to work with them to lobby for change. Regions have networks, and it may not matter if these are not to do with a particular innovatory area: for example, the NVQ co-ordinator may recognise some of the problems of being involved in change, and NCVQ and all the validating bodies have equal opportunities policies; as do the TECs.

Staff can work through national bodies such as the FEU, NIACE and NATFHE, through the governing body or through the LEA or through the community. The ideal is to have top-down support as a key part of overall strategic planning, and although this may not be immediately realisable, it may be possible to find internal networks which are supportive in other sections or departments.

It is important that multicultural education is integral rather than bolted-on to the curriculum. There is a need therefore to look at possible entry points to the curriculum and a few starting points might be:

- ☐ Active Tutorial: where multiculturalism could permeate each module;
- ☐ Communication Studies: which often includes Media Studies. Assignments could look at stereotypes;
- ☐ Subject: where there is a course review and monitoring which seeks to answer questions about who students are and how they differ from previous years. It is when questions of equality of opportunity are asked that a quality review is produced.

There may also be scope for colleges to 'twin' and share their expertise. This may take the form of students visiting each other or if this not viable, exchanging information using technology.

It is important to remember that:

- ☐ access to the curriculum is different from access to the institution;
- ☐ presenting work to the decision and policy makers of colleges is important but this should not only include lobbying Principals but also Section Heads of other disciplines;
- ☐ gaining encouragement by recognising that existing achievement, however small, may be helpful in itself and recognisable by comparing activity between individuals and institutions.

Chapter Five

CONCLUSIONS

Here we present conclusions that have been drawn from a large number of features of the AEMS Project.

1. National Management

The 'spider web' model using a national centre with nine regional arms had many advantages. The status and authority of a national project, supported by prestigious funding bodies has undoubtedly influenced senior education personnel, whose response may have been less welcoming if initiatives had been regional. Several co-ordinators stated that the affiliation to a London organisation attracted LEA members to a partnership commitment.

The Central AEMS office supported the regional group co-ordinators, and encouraged local interpretation of AEMS objectives.

For less experienced AEMS co-ordinators and project personnel, the national view of Black and cultural minority artists and curriculum developments provided by the AEMS team was invaluable.

2. School Management

The detailed case studies of South Glamorgan, Cheshire and Walsall illustrate three regional interpretations of the AEMS development plan, implemented with different levels of resources. They also illustrate three different approaches to developing artists as local educational resources, facilitating innovative curriculum initiatives and linking AEMS projects with the emergent National Curriculum.

2.1 New Methods of Working

The AEMS project stimulated a new management collaboration for two authorities whose advisers had previously worked individually. The expertise and authority of humanities advisers and multicultural advisers was channelled to a common goal of realising two years of AEMS projects in collectively targeted schools. Such management teams increased channels of communication with the authorities, consistently offered support to the regional co-ordinators and disseminated examples of professional training and teaching strategies throughout the authorities.

2.2 LEA and Arts Association Partnerships

The Case Study of South Glamorgan shows the impact on a political and policy making level of AEMS ideas on both LEA and Arts Association officers. Partnership advisers have stated categorically that AEMS allowed them to reinforce Education for All policies and provide imaginative and attractive ways of showing the possibilities of multicultural arts development.

2.3 Development of New Skills

The work of regional AEMS co-ordinators comprised of school-artist co-ordination, fund-raising, training, supporting other teaching staff in AEMS developments, monitoring and evaluation. All co-ordinators felt that their management capabilities in achieving these tasks has been significantly enhanced by the AEMS experience.

2.3 New Channels of Communication

A number of AEMS projects in Cheshire, Walsall and Huddersfield gave rise to contacts with new artists and multicultural community centres. For schools and colleges, AEMS offered new opportunities to develop links with communities and to develop the skills of local Black and cultural minority artists.

2.4 Confronting Racism

Several educators commented that the AEMS arts projects provided a practical illustration of equal opportunities and the realities of racism within and outside their educational institution. The interactive project of the Huddersfield Art and Design Department increased awareness of needs of Black students and improved Black and cultural minority recruitment.

The formation of a regional AEMS group could highlight overt and covert racism at every level of the educational institution. There were two examples of the first; anti-racist INSET training which provoked angry responses from local authority personnel. There have been several examples of overt racism within schools, where a pupil made racist comments during an artists' visit, despite that, in all of the school situations described, there were anti-racist codes of practice and strategies in place. However, a procedure which allowed such incidents to be used to explain further the school policy to the child perpetrators and the parents increased the confidence of teachers committed to equal opportunity and positive action on racism.

There are many examples where the AEMS project curriculum has enabled white students to engage and empathise with experiences of racism. The example of the Mary Seacole project in Walsall, where students devised a video drama based on Seacole, a Black nurse contemporary of Florence Nightingale, has had lasting impact on the young participants.

There is much empirical evidence of students who participated in AEMS of expanding their skills and perceptions and considering their own identity and that of others. Because the pattern of AEMS work was normally short term, it is not possible to reflect accurately the degree of personal change in students nor anticipate the level to which AEMS has eradicated overtly racist attitudes. Older students in further education have articulated how their attitudes have changed, and described new cultural encounters whether of a positive or a negative nature.

3. Multicultural Arts Curricula

AEMS produced many excellent models of pluralist arts practice, curriculum packs and videos. The twelve month Newham project developed ideas of a world art history drawing on the arts of Islam, Benin culture and British culture. The tri-lingual puppet project in Cardiff made creative use of oral traditions of Wales, England and India to explore the theme of heroes. The National Exhibition displayed a selection of artefacts and texts from regional groups over a 2 year period. Curriculum resources designed for English, Visual Art, Music and cross-curricular work were numerous. However, one of the weaknesses in some regional groups has been the failure to document projects and to retain artefacts, texts or teachers' evaluations to be used by future educators. One of the key functions of the regional groups was to disseminate models of good practice throughout the regions. Those groups with a previous history of documenting projects, whether by video recording, written reports or cassette projects could best capitalise on the opportunities afforded by AEMS projects. The National Exhibition and the two issues of the AEMS magazine provided a framework within which to view the results of AEMS projects and for local groups to have a sense of national perspective.

Specific working parties established in literature, music and carnival produced excellent curriculum material. Additionally the AEMS staff took part in early discussions of National Curriculum Working Groups and contributed to a greater understanding of multicultural issues. As regional groups matured, the co-ordinators also played a greater role in advising on curriculum development beyond their immediate regions.

4. Artists as Educational Resource

In 1987 AEMS organised the first national programme of training for artists wishing to work within education. The courses, attended by visual artists, musicians, storytellers, poets and actors, introduced the philosophy of AEMS, described the education context of the time and suggested approaches to project work.

The results of the artists' questionnaire show that almost all the artists who attended these courses have subsequently continued educational work. Several new networks across art-form have been created as a result of AEMS projects. In Cheshire, a new artists' co-operative has been established to promote South East Asian arts amongst parent governors.

Artists were unanimous in how important the AEMS philosophy was in schools. More than half of the artists commented that even after AEMS training, they were not quite prepared for some of the covert racism in their school experiences.

In South Glamorgan, AEMS artists were 'shadowed' by trainee artists, thus extending teaching skills to younger Black artists. There has been no previous comparable training for cultural minority artists, nor the opportunities to work in schools. A consideration for the future may be to expand further the skills of the 'first wave' of AEMS artists who have considerable experience. A second programme of AEMS training would once more describe the changed educational climate and help to identify new opportunities in some regions which have continued AEMS work.

5. Further Education

A number of specific conclusions have arisen from the case studies of AEMS in Further Education.

☐ There is a fundamental need to recognise that multiculturalism is a whole college responsibility regardless of the ethnic composition of students and staff. staff may have an existing equal opportunities policy or be working towards one, but there is a need for each college to include this area of work in their staff development programmes;

☐ The AEMS model should be extended to include business, tourism, engineering and catering programmes;

☐ Regional seminars could be planned with confidence in this area as there are a number of college staff in Britain who could disseminate their practice. This needs to be co-ordinated by a central body. These seminars should be aimed at including Principals and middle managers;

☐ Expertise in the field needs to be endorsed by pooling experiences around a group of colleges. These need not be geographically close but should be similar in size, courses offered, student population;

☐ Staff with existing experience need the provision of continuity. After an artist's placement, what happens? Staff and students need guidance in finding ways of motivating themselves and others;

☐ There needs to be a national listing of people involved in multiculturalism into an information folder. This would enhance the notion of networking;

☐ AEMS has worked with relatively few colleges. Further funds should be made available to enable AEMS and other agencies to continue to work in the Further Education sector;

☐ Validating bodies such as GNVQ, RSA and City and Guilds, need to be made more aware of their responsibility towards multiculturalism. Each college could influence the setting of national criteria;

☐ Colleges should find ways of creating links with the communities they serve. The content of courses should show evidence of community involvement;

☐ A monitoring and servicing role needs to be created for the Further Education sector. Colleges should bid to take on this responsibility within their region with initial funding. An external body should act in a co-ordinating role.

Chapter Six

OVERVIEW

The objectives of AEMS, formulated in the *Development Plan* of 1987 and revised in 1988 had their roots in the *Arts in Schools* project and the concurrent growth in the numbers of black artists working in new and traditional art forms. The interrelationship and consequences of these roots have been documented in the preceding chapters. This documentation began at the outset, for example we reproduce an intermediate appraisal by the Project Director in 1989.

This review implicitly shows the dialogue between teachers, students, artists, coordinator and LEA and RAA representatives. The following is suggested for discussion and action in order to continue growth and consolidate the project in the coming year.

Curriculum projects in the past have shown that bringing about the kind of change that AEMS is seeking is a long term process. It is often the case that the impact of projects which are initially successful can diminish if there is insufficient support and development. We must be aware of this in order to ensure that the developments initiated by AEMS are sustained well beyond the life of the project.

In 1987, when each LEA committed itself to the project, it was difficult to predict either how AEMS would develop or the way in which education in England and Wales might be reformed. Two years on, the project has an additional strategic role in ensuring that Central Government initiatives and polices reflect multicultural arts education.

It would be as well to remind ourselves however, that AEMS serves the spirit of the National Curriculum extremely well by providing coherence and progression through cross-phase, cross-curricular work.

At the simplest level of evaluation AEMS achieved all its objectives. It unquestionably explored and developed ways of delivering multicultural awareness in the arts curriculum. This was done by establishing models of good practice, providing information, new training initiatives for artists and teachers and, above all, by bringing a new and exciting wave of black artists and art forms into schools and communities where, previously, they had been virtually unknown.

The way AEMS did this by identifying and training Black and ethnic minority artists from a wide range of art forms, bringing them into active partnerships in schools and colleges, attracting large additional funding from local education authorities and the then Regional Arts Associations in urban and rural locations, in primary, secondary and further education institutions has been a remarkable achievement. The dramatic national exhibition involving many participants from all over Britain attracted major media attention and was in itself an impressive, positive evaluation of the project.

All these activities have been considered·in the preceding evaluation report and in this concluding section some of the key features that can now point the way to future development will be identified. Specifically they are:

- ☐ the role and influence of Black and ethnic minority artists;
- ☐ the new and previously inexperienced management issues that were solved;
- ☐ the curriculum issues that faced the schools and colleges;
- ☐ the political issues that surrounded the project;
- ☐ the theoretical issues that underpinned and guided the project.

1. The Role and Influence of the Artists

The project took the artists to places they had not and probably never could have reached before. It not only helped them to achieve new audiences; it enabled them to have a relationship with schools and colleges and with communities of a kind not normally enjoyed by artists. Most strikingly this occurred in the Menai residential week when Cheshire school children and their teachers worked and lived with Black artists.

The potential for the further creation of new audiences for black artists can only be guessed but must be considerable. Similarly the awareness of schools of the major contribution black artists can make to the curriculum and to learning generally must be very greatly enhanced.

The shadowing of Black artists by younger, inexperienced Black artists as in South Glamorgan offered yet a further gain in the build up of a *cadre* of capable Black artists.

Perhaps most importantly there has been developed a new and most effective training of Black and ethnic minority artists so that they may deliver their art forms to new audiences in a way that enhances personal rapport and involvement. Without this training much of the achievement could have been missed by inadvertence, inexperience or just the lack of specialist audience knowledge.

2. Management Issues

The success of the management strategies that brought artists, schools and colleges and, crucially, funding together is clearly evident. The ways in which this was achieved in various areas was often personal and even covert. But some features are clearly evident. They include the paramount influence of a national initiative legitimated by a prestigious body. Throughout the project this was perceived to be the Arts Council whose name rather than any specific funding or organisational pattern was highly significant. The need to gain national legitimacy was crucial but for the future there could be a range of possible sources.

As well as the need for legitimising the work there was clear evidence of the importance of some kind of management system to make schools aware of the opportunities, and also create mechanisms to identify, train and package Black artists. This latter is likely to remain essential until an artists' organisation can be set up to undertake the promotion, booking, agency and other management functions in educational contexts.

The then Regional Arts Associations and the Welsh Arts Council undertook some aspects of these management tasks and it was clear that, should they be willing to undertake them on a long term basis, they would be well equipped to do so as will their successors. The possibility of regional management initiatives undertaken by groups of the newly autonomous schools may also be an area of possible development. The reduction in power and responsibility of the LEAs make them a very unlikely source of continuing management delivery.

However the vital and inescapable aspect of finance cannot be ignored; the message of the project is that any management body must have effective strategies to achieve funding. The message is central, the convergence of national legitimation and financially capable management of activities has been an essential feature of the arts education developed by AEMS.

3. Curriculum Issues

It is clear that the contributions from Black and ethnic minority artists not only fitted into the curriculum, they also enhanced it. The National Curriculum in England and Wales evolved during the currency of the project (the Project Director herself playing a major part) and it is notable how readily the work of the project augmented the delivery of the curriculum orders for music, English, Art and Physical Education as well as adding an extra dimension to the work in history and geography. Perhaps even more importantly the project demonstrated the feasibility of incorporating (not simply adding) a truly multicultural dimension to a National Curriculum that, in its formulation, was at best an incompletely multicultural one. In so doing the project enhanced the perceptions and attitudes of many thousands of children and deepened and broadened their lives in a way that many had believed to be impossible in the National Curriculum of England and Wales.

The broadening of the curriculum not only occurred in schools but also in further education. A good example was the dramatic enhancement of the photography course at Dewsbury College of Education.

4. The Political Issues

It was here that the success of the project was most evident and the challenge 'popular latent racism' was most effective. The enthusiastic reception of the scheme and of the black and ethnic minority artists it brought was striking in many schools where little, if any, awareness of their work had existed before is the most telling achievement of the project. The willingness of Cheshire parents to send their children to the Menai Residential Week was a manifestation of this; the widespread and positive media response of the national exhibition another. But the project was not simply seeking an easier acceptance of black artists and their work; its approach was challenging — actively confronting racism as in the Mary Seacole project at Walsall. Here too it achieved impressive levels of understanding and recognition and changed attitudes in the process.

The socio-political challenge was clearly evident in many projects, for example in the South Glamorgan area. In all the artists played a key role far beyond that which they or anyone would normally have expected of artists. New curriculum dimensions were created at the interface of understanding and communication between black and white participants.

The influence on teachers' attitudes and thinking has also been powerful — not only have they discovered a way to enhance the curriculum but also a way to challenge both manifest and latent racism in urban and rural areas in a new and effective way. The project has provided an acceptable instrument of change not only in the classrooms but also in the staff rooms and in the communities. It has reinforced the committed anti-racist teachers and bought them new allies in their schools.

5. Theoretical Issues

The central theoretical issue underlying the project has been an implicit theory of social change. It asserts, that, with sensitive timing and strategies, the process of socialisation of young people can be guided and enlightened to the benefit of both individuals and communities. It is a theory that believes that even fundamental life attitudes and values are not simply created by some inevitable process of social and cultural reproduction but instead, as Bourdieu (1972) suggests, by a process that responds to sensitive intervention that is tuned to human needs and motivations.

Social and cultural change is of course inevitable but in the past planned interventions have usually been only attempted by politicians and, more recently, advertisers and media activists. The ensuing power has been used spasmodically and randomly and, as in pre-war Germany, it has been capable of producing appalling results when it has been abused.

Education has increasingly come to be seen as a key element in moving social change into desirable rather than undesirable directions; the AEMS project has shown that, in a small but crucially formative way, the mixture of the appropriate ingredients can help young people, parents and teachers, so that they can be bought to achieve, appreciate and respond to a truly multicultural educational experience. But even more importantly the project has shown that it is possible to internalise this experience to become part of the everyday thinking of young people with exciting prospects for use in their later lives.

But there is a still further gain. The project was underpinned by the prospect of creating new identities, inspired by the role model of the Black artists and, above all, the evidence that it was socially acceptable to White people and Black, many young Blacks were able to turn negative self-images into much more positive ones and achieve similar acceptability. Indeed for the first time many Black — and White — young people experienced and understood a positive Black self-image. This theme is well developed in an Arts Council funded book *Reconstructing the Black Image* (de la Mothe, 1993).

The Way Forward

Much of the future of the AEMS approach will be self generating — both in the schools and the communities where the initial work took place. And by word of mouth, publicity and the professional grapevine it will spread to other areas. But this is not enough to secure either the speed or permanency of the AEMS objectives. To ensure this it is necessary to ensure the existence of a body which gives legitimacy and an active management strategy to AEMS type activity. Such a body must also be able to seek out and distribute funding. In particular such a body must:

   ☐   ensure the maintenance and development of the AEMS Directory of
       Black and White Artists;

☐ to ensure the generation and, where appropriate, distribution of appropriate curriculum materials written in association with the artists and teachers for use before, during and after their visits;

☐ set up in-service courses for teachers and lecturers in which the artists play an active part.

☐ To ensure the training of black artists, particularly young artists, for work in education;

☐ to ensure that schools, teachers and artists enjoy support and advice, publicity and encouragement.

In this way an active, coherent rather than spasmodic future for AEMS type activities may occur and the crucial achievements reported here can be augmented and sustained, coherently and continuously.

However, it is only fitting that the final words go to the Director of the Project. Her interim conclusion, written in 1989, is still wholly fitting to the completed project.

> Finally, travelling as I do from one AEMS partnership Authority to another, I am often reminded of the West African and Caribbean character, Anancy. The traditional Anancy is a crisp, cool, calculating spider, a persuasive, inventive, anarchic spider man. He holds some reservations, makes selective allowances, challenges assumptions and questions value judgements. He is a moral advocate, a politician, an educator. He unlocks the imagination through his range of guises and different languages of expression.

> When I observe workshops, I see students, teachers and artists engaged seriously and sensitively in issues which would make Anancy pause, draw breath, adopt an appropriate disguise and create a tale based on what he saw. He would then take this tale everywhere, exciting everyone in the re-telling. Just like Anancy, the AEMS project endeavours to work at many levels and have a lasting effect.

> I have given my interpretation of the project — the journey and critical eyes are yours.

> *Maggie Semple, Director, AEMS*

References

Bourdieu, P (1977) 'Cultural Reproduction and Social Reproduction' in Karabel, J. and Halsey, A.H. (eds) *Power and Ideology in Education,* Oxford: University Press

de la Mothe (1993) *Reconstructing the Black Image*, Stoke-on-Trent: Trentham Books

Semple, M (1989) *Arts Education for a Multicultural Society*, Interim Review, London: Arts Council

---

Copies of the 1991 AEMS Directory of Artists are still available at £6.00 (incl. p&p) from:

Kitty Solomons
Barnet Professional Development Centre
451 High Road
Finchley
London N12 0AS

Tel: 0181 359 3874
Fax: 0181 359 3872